Ludwig van Beethoven

EIGHTH AND NINTH SYMPHONIES

in Full Orchestral Score

Dover Publications, Inc., New York

This Dover edition, first published in 1976, reproduces all
the music from the separate volumes of the symphonies edited
by Max Unger and published by Ernst Eulenburg, Ltd., London, n.d. In the present volume, the introductions by Wilhelm
Altmann (in the Eulenburg volumes these are in their original
German with French and English translations) are reproduced
in English only—but in a totally new translation—while the
Editor's Preface (Revisionsbericht) to the Ninth Symphony,
originally in German only, also appears in a specially prepared
new English translation. A new translation of the vocal texts
of the Ninth Symphony is also included.

International Standard Book Number: 0-486-23380-4
Library of Congress Catalog Card Number: 76-14017

Manufactured in the United States of America
Dover Publications, Inc.
180 Varick Street
New York, N.Y. 10014

Contents

Symphony No. 8 in F Major, Op. 93

The original MS (unusually for Beethoven, without a dedication) is in the Music Division of the Prussian State Library in Berlin; it is titled: "Sinfonia Lintz im Monath October 1812." The work was begun immediately after the Seventh, surely before the Seventh was completed. (In his letter of June 1, 1815, to Peter Salomon, Beethoven calls this a smaller symphony in contrast to the great A major, but otherwise he was especially fond of it.)

Drafts of it are found in the so-called Petter sketchbook, which in Thayer's opinion was begun as early as 1809, whereas Nottebohm, probably more correctly, dates the earliest entries to 1811. These sketches for all the movements precede sketches for the piano and violin sonata published as Op. 96, which was played at the home of Archduke Rudolph by December 29, 1812. When Beethoven wrote, in a letter received by Breitkopf & Härtel on June 1, 1812, "I am writing 3 new symphonies, one of which is already completed," the second one must naturally have been the one published as the Eighth. It was also one of the two "entirely new" symphonies that Beethoven placed at the disposal of the state attorney Varena in Graz in February or March 1813 for a charity concert, although he revoked the offer on May 27, writing: "I would gladly have sent you 2 entirely new symphonies of mine, but my present situation unfortunately compels me to think of myself, and I cannot tell whether I may not have to leave here soon as a fugitive; for this you can thank the excellent princes who [by reducing their promised subsidies] have made it impossible for me to work as usual on behalf of good and useful causes." This F major symphony must have already been written out in parts by April 18, 1813, since on that date Beethoven wrote to his friend Zmeskall: "Perhaps the symphonies will be rehearsed at the Archduke's tomorrow."

The first public performance did not take place until February 27, 1814, at one of Beethoven's own concerts.

Along with a dozen other works, including the symphony in A, the Eighth was sold on April 29, 1815, to the Viennese publisher S. A. Steiner with rights for all countries except England.

The title of the original edition, in parts, reads: "Achte Grosse Sinfonie in F dur für 2 Violinen, 2 Violen, 2 Flauten, 2 Oboen, 2 Clarinetten, 2 Fagott, 2 Horn, 2 Trompeten, Pauken, Violoncello und Basso von Ludwig van Beethoven 93tes Werk. Eigenthum der Verleger. Wien, im Verlag bei S. A. Steiner & Comp." (publication number 2571). The lithographed score, published at the same time, was later replaced by an engraved one issued by the same firm, which had meanwhile been taken over by Tobias Haslinger, whose name appeared on the imprint.

Beethoven did not add the metronome marks till later, at the same time as those for Symphonies 1 through 7; all these were published in the supplement to the *Allgemeine musikalische Zeitung*, Leipzig, of December 17, 1817.

Berlin

WILHELM ALTMANN

Symphony No. 9 in D Minor, Op. 125

On June 1, 1812, the Leipzig publishing house of Breitkopf & Härtel received a letter from Beethoven, in which he wrote: "I am writing 3 new symphonies, one of which is already completed." In the so-called Petter sketchbook, which contains the drafts for the symphonies published as the Seventh, Op. 92, and the Eighth, Op. 93, both probably begun in 1811, there is to be found (see Gustav Nottebohm, *Zweite Beethoveniana*, p. 111) among sketches for the second movement of Op. 92 the words "second symphony D minor," and among sketches for Op. 93 the remark "Symphony in D minor—third symphony." But this sister symphony of Opp. 92 and 93 was never carried through. In a sketchbook of 1815 (Nottebohm, *op. cit.*, p. 157), after the last drafts for the piano and cello sonata Op. 102, No. 2, the following fugue theme occurs among other sketches, of which only some were adopted:

This contains the germ of the theme of the second movement of the Ninth Symphony. But Beethoven did not pursue this further for the moment.

After considering a B minor symphony very briefly in 1815, Beethoven decided seriously in 1817 to proceed with not just one, but two new symphonies. While the second one also was still on his mind in 1822, he started serious work in 1817 (along with his work on the large-scale piano sonata Op. 106) only on that symphony[1] which was later to give rise to the one published as the Ninth (Nottebohm, *op. cit.*, pp. 157 ff.), but did not progress much beyond drafts of the first two movements; yet it can clearly be seen that the finale was to be purely instrumental, and there was no thought yet of using Schiller's ode "To Joy." But on a sheet that can be dated to the first half of 1818, we already read: "Adagio Cantique. Pious song in a symphony in the old modes—Lord God, we praise Thee—hallelujah—either on its own or as introduction to a fugue. Perhaps the entire second [!] symphony to be characterized in this way, with the vocal parts entering in the last movement or even in the Adagio. The orchestral violins, etc., to be multiplied by ten in the last movement. Or the Adagio will somehow be repeated in the last movement, and only then will the vocal parts enter gradually—in the Adagio text, Greek myth, Cantique Ecclesiastique—in the Allegro, celebration of Bacchus." Thus we see that even then he had two symphonies in mind. We cannot follow the phases by which they later coalesced into one.

These drafts were set aside in favor of other works, the piano sonatas Opp. 109, 110 and 111, the overture Op. 124 and, above all, the Missa Solemnis, and were only resumed in a new sketchbook of 1822.[2] He was still thinking of two symphonies. For a while he wanted to use the 1815 fugal theme, which he had destined for the second movement in 1817, for the finale of one of the symphonies. Drafts of an Adagio, however, are lacking in this 1822 sketchbook, though it does already contain, with the heading "Finale" (for the second, "German" symphony), the theme:

This Schiller text had already engaged Beethoven's attention. In the so-called Petter sketchbook, probably of 1811, we already find an essentially different C major theme for it (Thayer-Deiters-Riemann, *Beethovens Leben*, vol. III, p. 153) with the following remarks: "Freude, schöner Götterfunken, Tochter. Work out overture. Freude, schöner Götterfunken,

---

[1] In contrast to this one, he sometimes called the other symphony he was working on "allemande." We shall see that the one that became the Ninth was destined upon completion for performance in England, although an instrumental finale was surely desired there.

[2] Nottebohm, p. 164, calls attention to the following notice in the Leipzig *Allgemeine musikalische Zeitung* of January 22, 1823: "Beethoven has now completed his second grand Mass. He is said to be working on a new symphony at present."

Tochter aus Elysium. Detached sentences like: Princes are beggars, etc., not the whole thing. Detached sentences from Schiller's Joy made into a whole."

As Nottebohm has shown, the year 1823 was chiefly devoted to the Ninth Symphony; not only was the first movement completed, but the three others were begun and composed, except for the instrumental introduction of the Finale. A draft of the second movement was ready by about August; the Adagio, of which the melody of the middle section was created first, by about October. As for the Finale, for which the melody later used in the last movement of the string quartet Op. 132 was seriously considered for a while, the choral part and the instrumental variations on the joy theme that precede it were written first. The sketches for the symphony must have been finished at the end of 1823 or at the very beginning of 1824, the score by about February 1824.

Its completion is related beyond any doubt to the request for a symphony made by the Philharmonic Society in London after a resolution of November 10, 1822; the payment was to be 50 pounds. The mediator was probably Ferdinand Ries, to whom Beethoven, who had been ailing half a year, had written on April 6, 1822: "What would the Philharmonic Society offer me for a symphony?" On December 22, 1822, he wrote: "I am pleased to accept the offer to write a new symphony for the Philharmonic Society." In his letter to Ries of the fifth of February (not September, as is sometimes erroneously stated), 1823, we read: "I still have no further news about the symphony. Meanwhile, you can count on it firmly. I have made the acquaintance here of a very charming educated man, who is employed at our Imperial embassy in London; he will undertake later to help deliver the symphony from here to you in London, so that it will reach London quickly. If I were not so poor that I must live by my pen, I would take nothing from the Philharmonic Society, but as it is I must wait until the fee for the symphony is announced here." By February 25, 1823, Beethoven still had had no word from London on the fee to be expected, as we learn from his letter to Ries. When he wrote Ries on April 25, "You will receive the symphony very soon," excusing the delay in delivery on the grounds of present necessity to compose only in return for income, and when he wrote Archduke Rudolph on July 1, 1823,

"I am now writing a new symphony for England, for the Philharmonc Society, and I hope to complete it in two weeks," he was being premature about its completion.

But this was accomplished in August. From Beethoven's letter to Ries of September 5, 1823 (Kalischer No. 961; No. 962, which Kalischer prints under the same date, was really written on February 5), we learn that the score of the symphony had been completed by the copyist in the last few days and that the composer was merely waiting for a good opportunity to send it off.[3] But it was not until after the Ninth had been performed in Vienna on May 7, 1824,[4] that it was sent to London, where it was not heard until March 21, 1825.

On March 15, 1824, Beethoven offered the symphony and the Missa Solemnis to the Leipzig music publisher H. A. Probst, whose firm was later taken over by F. Kistner. He wrote: "A long new symphony, which has a finale in which vocal parts enter, soloists and choruses, to the words of Schiller's immortal song to joy, in the manner of my piano fantasy with chorus, but on a much larger scale; my fee would be 600 gulden in Convention coinage. Of course, I must make the stipulation that the symphony should not be published until July of next year, 1825, but in compensation for this long delay I would be happy to supply you with the piano reduction at no additional charge." Since by March 19 the offer had not been accepted as it stood, on May 20 Beethoven (who had perhaps already negotiated fruitlessly with Viennese publishers) turned to B. Schott's Sons in Mainz, who had asked him for pieces, but even though this firm was perfectly willing to take the Mass especially, as well as the symphony, and had already made an advance payment, still on August 28, 1824, Beethoven gave Probst in Leipzig, who was trying to renew contact with him, hopes of getting the symphony, writing: "In regard to the symphony, which is the largest in scale I have written, and for which even foreign artists have made me proposals, it would be possible for you to have it;

[3] On September 8, Beethoven wrote to Franz Christian Kirchhoffer in Vienna, who was to send the symphony to Ries in London: "You will receive the score of the symphony in two weeks at most." But he had to review the copyist's work thoroughly.

[4] In his edition of Beethoven's letters Kalischer erroneously dated to 1825 the letter to the copyist Wolanek (vol. V, p. 101) that includes the phrase: "Since I cannot complete the scoring of the Finale before Easter."

but you must decide very quickly, because I already have a part of the fee, though I could give this man other compositions for it. Although God blesses me especially (since I help likewise wherever I can) and I never lack for publishers, still I want you to know that I like simplicity in dealings. By giving that man other pieces, I would have no further effort in that direction and could leave the symphony for you, but it should not be published before July of next year. If you consider the time needed in the interim for engraving and correcting it, the delay is not so great. Meanwhile, do not abuse my confidence, and make no use of these remarks of mine in conversations with others." We do not know whether Probst refused this arrangement; at any rate, B. Schott's Sons got the symphony on February 4, 1825 (Kalischer, *Beethoven's Letters*, V, p. 105), in a copy corrected by Beethoven with which he was far from pleased.

The symphony was published in score and parts (publication number 2322) in the second half of 1826 with the title: "Sinfonie mit Schluss-Chor über Schillers Ode 'An die Freude' für grosses Orchester, 4 Solo- und 4 Chorstimmen componiert und Seiner Majestät dem Konig von Preussen Friedrich Wilhelm III in tiefster Ehrfurcht zugeeignet von Ludwig van Beethoven. 125tes Werk. Eigenthum der Verleger. Mainz und Paris bey B. Schott's Söhnen."

The original MS of the score, which has numerous alterations and also deletions in the Scherzo, is in the Music Division of the Prussian State Library. Bound together (and once in the possession of Anton Schindler) are the first three movements and a fragment of the Finale, from the "Allegro assai vivace alla marcia" to the 3/2 "Andante maestoso" (pp. 302 to 328 in the present volume). The sections that complete this fragment, partially written on larger-size paper, did not enter the Library's collection until 1902, when the Artaria Collection was acquired. This score is disfigured here and there by dynamic markings or pizzicati entered in red pencil. At the beginning of the first movement Beethoven added in pencil: "108 oder 120 Mälzel," but later in the printed version he changed this to "♪= 88." The D major section of the Scherzo (p. 223 in this volume) is written in 2/4 time, but Beethoven wrote the following indication for the copyist: "To be written throughout in ₵ time; a whole measure to be made out of half measures, e.g.

He also added numbers to clarify the ₵ time division for the copyist. The coda of the Scherzo (p. 232 in this volume) is lacking. Possibly it was not added until shortly before printing. In the Finale the contrabassoon part,[5] present in the printed edition, is missing up to the 6/8 "alla marcia" (p. 302 in this volume); the clarinets in B-flat are entered below the contrabass part, after their original version was crossed out, until in the first D major "Allegro assai" in ₵ time (p. 273 in this volume) they are replaced by clarinets in A. Where the 1st bassoon enters in that section (p. 271 in this volume), Beethoven added in pencil: "2do fag. col B[asso]," but either this was not heeded, or else he changed his mind again during publication. When the bass vocalist enters with "O Freunde," the MS has only   that is, there

is no grace note before the *e*, nor do we find the *c*-sharp that may be sung instead of the *e*. After this bass solo Beethoven wrote a note to himself to the effect that the solo parts and the chorus would now need new lines on the paper, and started using much larger sheets, entering the vocal parts below the contrabass line. Of the 43 instrumental measures preceding the tenor solo in the 6/8 "Allegro assai vivace alla marcia" (p. 302 in this volume), only the first 12 are in the original MS. In the repeat of the chorus' "Deine Zauber binden wieder, was die Mode streng geteilt, alle Menschen werden Brüder, wo dein sanfter Flügel" (pp. 325 ff. in this edition), only the soprano line is written out, with "come sopra" above and below it. The D major "Allegro energico sempre ben marcato" (p. 337 in this volume) is in 3/2 time, not 6/4 as later in the printed edition. In the D major section "Tempo I [Allegro ma non tanto]" (p. 369 in this volume), after "weilt" one instrumental measure is missing (and two occur in a different version), and so are the seven measures of the chorus: "Deine Zauber, deine Zauber binden wieder, was die Mode streng geteilt." Beethoven crossed out the indication "Prestissimo" at the end (p. 389 in this volume) and replaced it by "Presto," but restored the "Prestissimo" in the printed version. It should be expressly stated here that this orig-

---

[5] A contrabassoon part in Beethoven's own hand is in the Music Division of the Prussian State Library in Berlin.

inal MS[6] is not as significant for a new critical edition as the fair copies done by copyists and carefully checked by Beethoven[7] and the first printed edition that incorporates his revisions.

Beethoven established the metronome marks in the fall of 1826 and sent them to the publishers on October 13. In the score published by Schott the metronome mark of the D major section of the Scherzo is incorrectly given as 𝅝 = 116 instead of 𝅗𝅥 = 116.

WILHELM ALTMANN

---

[6] The Leipzig firm of Kistner & Siegel published a facsimile of it in 1925.

[7] In addition to the two copies sent to Schott and to the London Philharmonic Society, an important one is the fair copy made for King Friedrich Wilhelm III of Prussia as the dedication copy, with a title page in Beethoven's own hand; since 1860 this has been in the Music Division of the Prussian Royal, later State, Library in Berlin.

Editor's Preface to Ninth Symphony

In preparing a critical edition of the Ninth Symphony, it would be possible to consult—in addition to the original autograph MS, now in the Berlin State Library, and the first edition—several MS copies corrected by Beethoven: the engraving copy, still in the possession of B. Schott's Sons, the first publishers of the work, as well as some other copies that the composer ordered for various reasons before the printing of the symphony. But apart from the fact that these MS scores are preserved in far-flung cities —Berlin, Aachen, London—it is very questionable whether the result would be worth the effort involved, since it is to be doubted that the composer, always hard-pressed by new assignments, could have afforded the concentration necessary to check them accurately line by line. Without question, the most important aids are the engraving copy and the first printing, although even they are not free of errors and inaccuracies, and Beethoven did not read the proofs of the first edition himself. But according to Schindler's biography, 3rd ed., vol. II, p. 151, he was so satisfied with the work that the Frankfurt musician Ferdinand Kessler did in this regard that he wrote him a letter of commendation.

The first edition and the engraving copy used to prepare it were the principal source texts for the present edition. I checked the first edition myself as thoroughly as possible. Mr. Franz Wilms, artistic adviser on the staff of B. Schott's Sons, was most cooperative in comparing a considerable number of unclear passages in the first edition against the engraving copy. I thank him heartily here for his unsparing effort and care. The autograph MS in Berlin is next in importance after the engraving copy and the first edition; it is still pretty far away from the definitive version. Apart from other divergencies in the text, several passages are lacking in it, as Wilhelm Altmann has already partially indicated in his introduction, page xi: mm. 13–44 (composed later) of the B-flat major march in the last movement; the last five measures of the Adagio ma non troppo, B-flat major, $\frac{3}{2}$, in the same movement (probably a sheet of the MS is lost); the coda of the scherzo (a double sheet, which Schindler, the first owner of the autograph MS after Beethoven, gave to Ignaz Moscheles in London soon after the composer's death and up to a few years ago was in the possession of Edward Speyer in Shenley); and the last repetition of the words "Deine Zauber binden wieder, was die Mode streng geteilt," as already noted by Altmann on p. xi above. Also missing are the parts of the contrabassoon and most of the trombones; they were composed afterward and written down on other sheets. (The contrabassoon part is also in the Prussian State Library today; the trombone parts missing in the full-score MS are in Mr. Hans C. Bodmer's major collection of Beethoven MSS in Zurich.) Despite all this, the autograph MS was also of importance in comparing numerous passages.

The present volume is not intended as a reconstitution of the "original text" in the strict sense, but as a practical edition that comes as close as possible to the composer's intentions. (A true "original-text" edition would end up merely as a reproduction of the autograph MS, which was still very incomplete.) Therefore, in this Preface I cannot indicate every supplied phrasing or dynamic mark or every error in writing or engraving in the engraving copy and the first edition. Instead, I point out only large errors in writing or engraving that have been handed down, and the more significant doubtful readings.

First movement, m. 130 (p. 125): In the first edition, all eight 16th-notes in the 2nd violin part

are given an octave too high. The autograph MS and the engraving copy show the correct position.

M. 138 (p. 128): All three sources have f in the winds and timpani, but $f\!f$ in the strings. In our edition, the $f\!f$ has been extended to all the parts.

M. 217 (p. 138): All three sources, and later publications, have an incorrect note in the 2nd violins and violas. A comparison with the woodwinds will confirm this:

Wrong: Right:

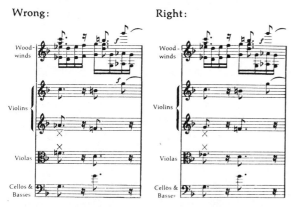

(Compare Vincenzo Tommasini's article "Quelques erreurs dans des partitions célèbres corrigées par Toscanini" in the January 1936 *Revue musicale*.) It is amazing how long this slip of the pen on Beethoven's part has been perpetuated in published scores!

Second movement, m. 70 (p. 196): In the autograph MS, horns 1 & 2 have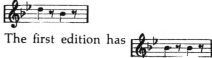

In the first edition the preceding *eb*" is resolved into *d*":

Apparently Beethoven entered the note afterward into the engraving copy, but a little unclearly. The second version, adopted in all publications, is probably correct.

Mm. 378 & 379 (p. 218): In the first edition the tie between the two *c♯*' in the viola part is lacking, but it is in the autograph MS and was probably intended by the composer.

Mm. 414 & 415 (p. 222): The famous first entry of the bass trombone

is completely lacking in the autograph MS; the engraving copy and the first edition indicate only >*p* (without *ff* or). Since a dynamic mark for the onset is obligatory, our edition adopts the usual reading.

Fourth movement, mm. 3 & 4 (p. 265): The autograph MS gives the flutes

In the engraving copy and the first edition, they have

It is hard to determine what Beethoven meant. Possibly the version in the engraving copy is due to a mistake of the copyist. Therefore, our edition goes back to the autograph MS, which was also followed in this passage by the complete works edition. Of course, the question is not very important, since the effect produced by the two readings is practically the same.

Mm. 9 & 10 (p. 176): On the discrepancy between the autograph MS on the one hand, and the engraving copy and first edition on the other, with regard to the word "Freunde" in the bass soloist's first entry, see p. xiii of the introduction in this volume.

M. 53 (p. 306): The autograph MS and the engraving copy give the tenor soloist

The first edition has

which is thus incorrect. The passage is given correctly in probably all later publications.

M. 45 (p. 348): The autograph MS gives the 2nd violins

whereas the engraving copy has

Our edition follows the autograph MS here.

Mm. 10–16 (pp. 339 & 340): Here at any rate the engraver of the first edition overlooked a correction made by Beethoven. In m. 11, the engraving copy had originally indicated on the bassoon staff: "Due Fagotti col Tenore." Beethoven crossed this out in pencil and wrote beneath it hastily: "I col Tenore II c Basso." But the engraver followed the *deleted* indication, so that the first edition gives this version of the passage (we include the two preceding measures):

instead of the following:

The second reading is adopted in the complete works edition as well. Unfortunately the autograph MS affords no help in this passage because there is an erasure where the words occur that indicate the role of the bassoons in abbreviated fashion.

Mm. 33–46 (pp. 345–348): According to the engraving copy and the first edition, the 2nd bassoon plays in unison with the 1st. In the engraving copy the passage (the context is included here) reads:

On the other hand, Beethoven indicated at the beginning of this passage in the autograph MS, obviously correctly:

c B 2 do Fag.

and entered only the 1st bassoon in the following measures. Thus the passage is incorrect in the engraving copy and in the first edition, but correct in the later score publications, which here follow the autograph MS.

M. 104 (p. 359): An error in the autograph MS perpetuated in the engraving copy, first edition and modern editions: the woodwinds already have the c, the dominant seventh of the subdominant, on the first quarter-beat; the altos and violas, however, still have c♯, the third of the dominant, on the first quarter and do not change to c until the fourth quarter. The passage

should read, not

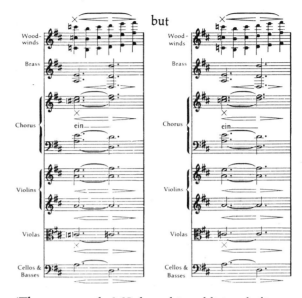

(The autograph MS has this additional divergence from the engraving copy and the first edition in the viola part: 𝄢 .)

This very unpleasant error has naturally already come to the attention of other conductors besides Toscanini (see *Revue musicale*, loc. cit.), but has not yet disappeared from the editions of score and parts.

M. 61 (p. 370): In the text of the last repetition of the words "Deine Zauber binden wieder, was die Mode streng geteilt," the first edition of the score and of the parts contains the reading "frech" (impudently) instead of "streng" (rigidly). Near the end of his 1870 book on Beethoven, Richard Wagner passionately upheld this "frech," asserting that in the "almost furiously threatening unison" the composer was not satisfied with the word "streng" for "his angry expression" and thus "from the perfection of his own power" wrote in that "frech." The question was long debated in the literature without a real decision. Many important conductors concurred with Wagner's view, and the alteration at this high point was often performed. Since I came to have certain reservations about the idea of the Bayreuth master, several years ago, through the kindness of the present owners of the firm B. Schott's Sons, I obtained permission to examine the engraving copy. It turned out that the eight measures in question, which do not yet exist in the autograph MS, were attached to the copyist's MS at a later time: they are written in a different hand from that of the MS of the entire last movement and already contain the expression "frech."

The error no doubt got into the first edition in the following manner: Beethoven had given the eight subsequently composed measures, with the correct Schiller text, to a copyist who was unfamiliar with his writing of words. This man read the word "stre – – ng" as "fre – – ch." (Under long notes and tied or slurred passages, the composer separated the final consonants from the beginning of a word by a dash of the appropriate length.) This is not surprising in itself, since even people more highly educated than simple copyists have had great trouble with Beethoven's writing, and actually those two words in his hand are fairly similar. This copyist obviously looked over the double sheet too quickly and probably attached it to the MS score himself without observing the mistake. Then the engraver faithfully entered the "frech" onto his plates. Perhaps this escaped the notice of the proofreader Kessler also, but even if he saw it, the engraving copy absolved him of the responsibility.

There are good internal musical reasons, as well, to prove that in this passage Beethoven did not want the word "frech." First of all, he would doubtless have also used intensified dynamic marks to make clear the "incredible climax" and the "angry expression" of which Wagner speaks. But the dynamics are the same as in the next-to-the-last passage in which these words are set, and the instrumentation, too, which is hardly changed, gives no climactic effect to the last repetition. (More can be read about this in the essay "On the Disputed Text Passage in the Ninth Symphony," which I published in No. 7 of the 19th annual series of *Die Musik*.) Another especially significant factor is that, apart from the engraving copy, the contemporary MSS, in so far as they have been preserved and can thus be examined, do not have "frech" in the questionable passage; compare also the article "Subsequent Evidence on the Ninth Symphony," which Otto Baensch, first an opponent but later a partisan of the conviction here expressed, contributed to the fourth annual volume of the *Neues Beethoven-Jahrbuch*.

Zurich

Dr. Max Unger

Translation of Vocal Texts in Last Movement

(Extracts from Friedrich Schiller's "To Joy")

Page 284, Recitativo, words by Beethoven: O friends, not these tones! rather, let us begin to sing more pleasant and more joyful ones.

Pages 286 ff.:
Joy, beautiful divine spark, maiden from Elysium: we are intoxicated with fire, heavenly being, as we enter your sanctuary! Your spells reunite what fashion has rigidly sundered; all men become brothers wherever your gentle wing reposes.

Let whoever has gained the great stake and has become friend of a friend, let whoever has won a lovely woman, add his jubilation to ours! Yes, whoever in the world merely calls a soul his own! And let whoever has never been able to do so, steal away in tears from this company.

All beings drink joy at the breasts of nature; all good men, all evil men follow her trail of roses. She gave us kisses and the vine, a friend tested in death; sexual pleasure was granted to the worm, and the cherub stands in the sight of God!

Pages 305 ff.:
Happily as His suns fly through heaven's splendid field, run your course, brothers, joyfully as a hero to victory.

Joy, beautiful divine spark . . . (etc.) gentle wing reposes.

Pages 329 ff.:
Be embraced, O millions. This kiss for the whole world! Brothers! above the starry tent a loving Father must dwell. You fall down, O millions? Do you have a presentiment of the Creator, O world? Seek Him above the starry tent! Over stars He must dwell.

Pages 337 ff.:
{Joy, beautiful divine spark . . . (etc.) sanctuary!
{Be embraced, O millions . . . (etc.) whole world!
You fall down . . . (etc.) Father must dwell.

Pages 360 ff.:
Joy . . . (etc.) wing reposes.

Pages 375 ff.:
Be embraced . . . (etc.). Joy . . . (etc.)!

Symphony No. 8

I

Allegro vivace e con brio (♩.=69)

L. van Beethoven, Op. 93
1770 - 1827

4

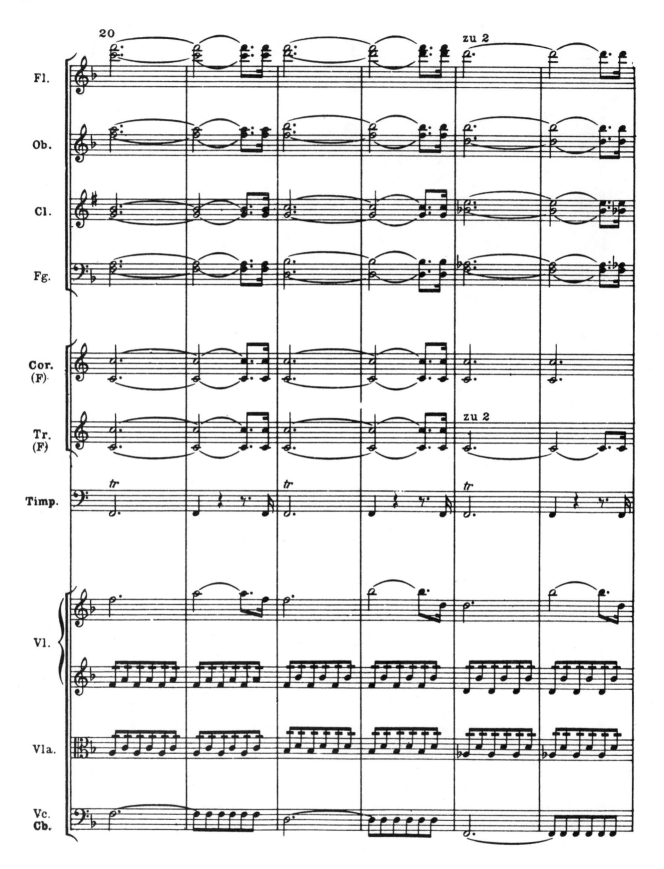

14

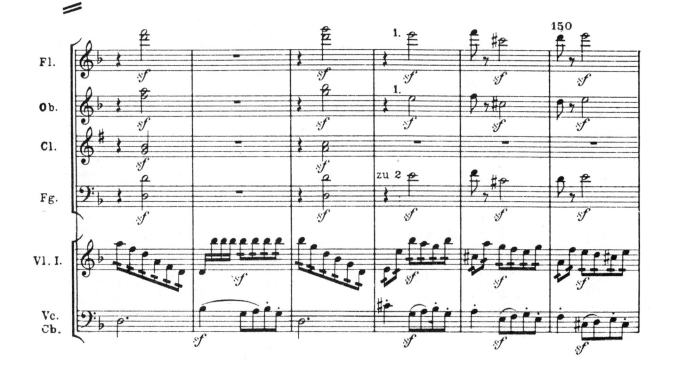

24

28

280

34

830

38

II

Allegretto scherzando (♪ = 88)

44

48

50

III

Tempo di Menuetto (♩=126)

56

58

Menuetto da Capo al Fine.

IV

Allegro vivace (♩=84)

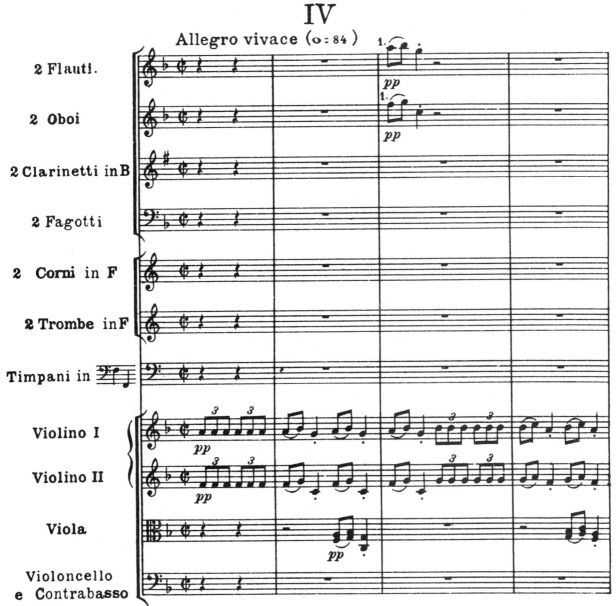

66

68

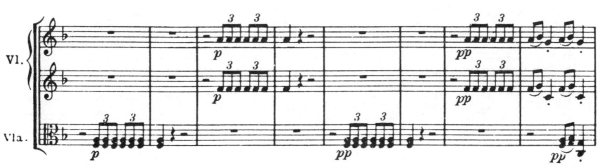

70

74

76

83

86

88

93

100

440

104

106

108

Symphony № 9

I

L. van Beethoven, Op.125
1770-1827

112

113

118

120

124

125

126

[V]
seems ready to break here
Goes through B-flat, upward in
parallel sixths

128

129

130

134

136

142

144

152

162

380

166

168

170

172

174

176

What did scales lead to at 102?

Resolves ♪♪♪ into rising scale, washes out into sequence.

178

490

180

ritard. a tempo

ritard. a tempo

188

190

191

192

196

Sequence of fifths; based on basic material of fugue.

disguised continuation of sequence

Six bar grouping | 4 bar grouping

Double counterpoint at the octave (flipping of parts)

200

202

1.
190
Fl.
Ob.
Cl.
Fg.
Timp.
Vl.
Vla.
Vc.
Cb.
one note changed
6 bar unit
200
Cor.
(B)
pedal

204

Subjects enter every two bars

270

210

290

212

Theme II

Same bass for recap. As opening.

214

216

218

220

Coda pag. 232

stringendo il tempo

222

223

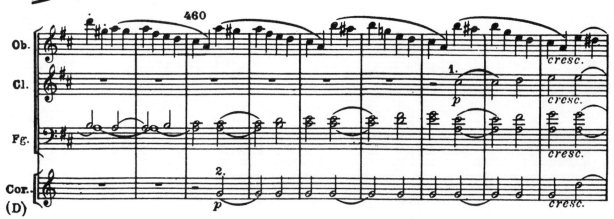

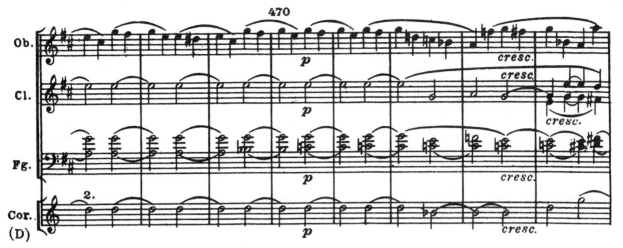

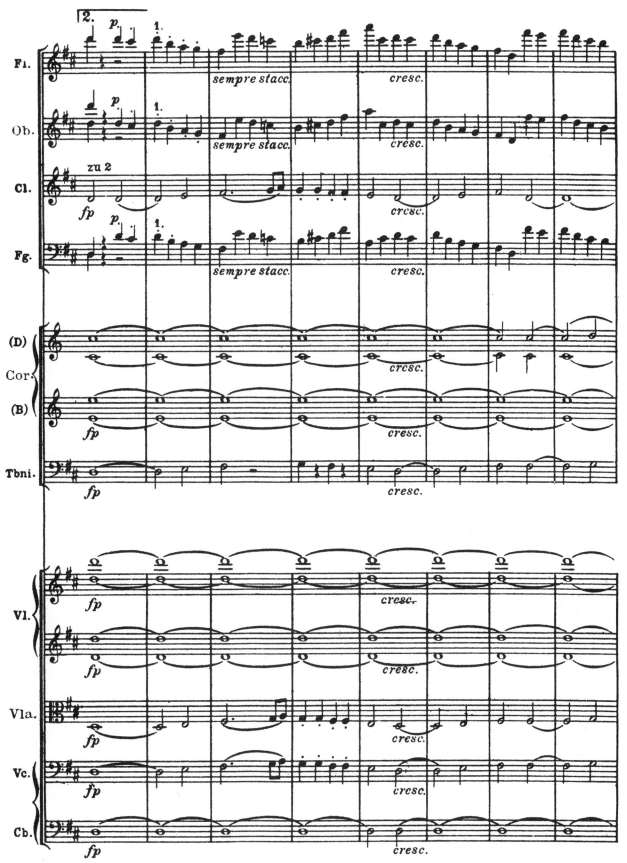

poco ritard.

Scherzo (Pag. 190) *da capo al ✛* (Pag. 220.)
e poi la Coda (Pag. 232.)

234

III

Adagio molto e cantabile ♩=60

Tempo I.

242

Andante.

244

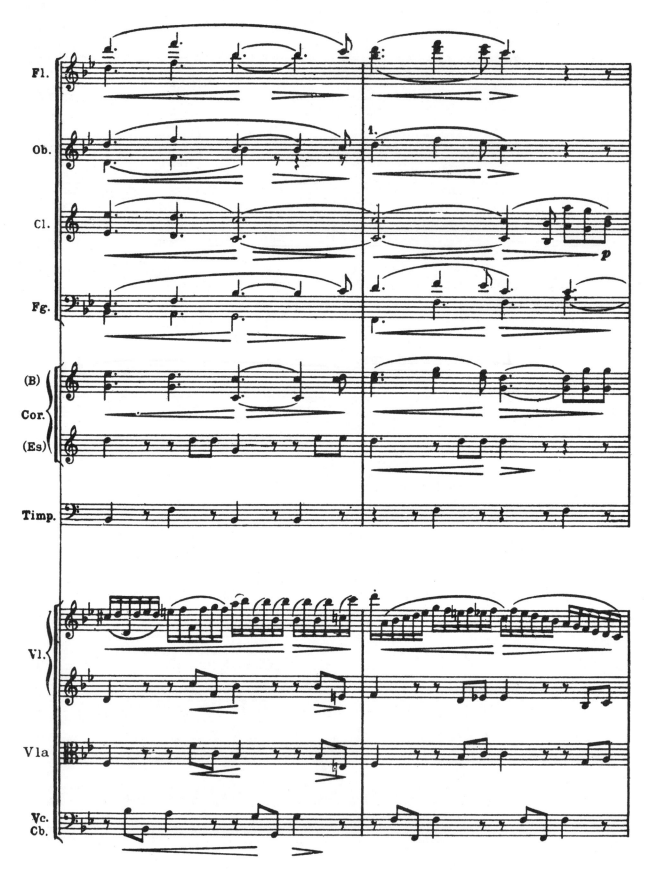

247

256

259

IV

Presto. (♩.=96)

266

f Selon le caractère d'un recitative, mais in tempo.

Allegro ma non troppo. (♩ = 88)

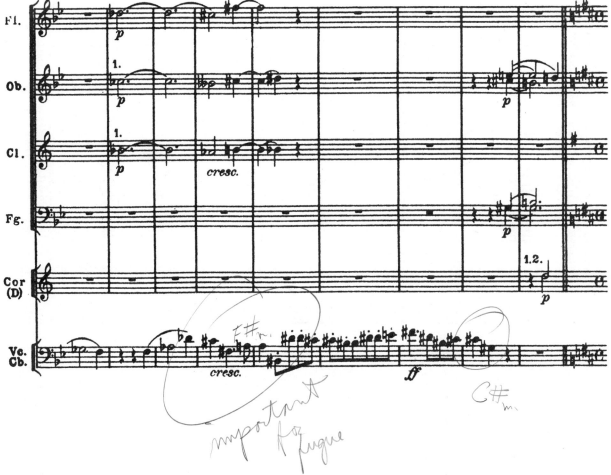

274

276

282

284

Recitativo.

O Freun - - - de, nicht die - se Tö-ne!

Recit.

20

Vl.

colla voce

colla voce

Vla.

colla voce

Brt.
Solo

son-dern laßt uns an - - - - ge-neh-me-re än-

Vc.
Cb.

colla voce

Fl.

Ob.

Cl
(A)

Fg.

zu 2

Cfg.

Cor.
(D)

zu 2

Tr.
(D)

Timp.

Vl.

Vla.

Brt.
Solo

ad lib

stimmen, und freu - - - - - - - den-vol-le-re.

Vc.
Cb.

Tochter aus E - ly - si-um, wir be-tre-ten feu-er-trunken, Himmli-sche, dein Hei-lig-tum!

Dei-ne Zau-ber binden wieder, was die Mo-de streng geteilt; al - le Menschen werden Brüder,

288

80

Chor

le Menschen werden Brü-der, wo dein sanfter Flü-gel weilt.

le Menschen werden Brü-der, wo dein sanfter Flü-gel weilt.

le Menschen werden Brü-der, wo dein sanfter Flü-gel weilt.

Wer ein hol-des Weib er-rungen, mische seinen Ju-bel ein! Ja, wer auch nur ei - ne See-le

wer ein hol-des Weib er-rungen, mische seinen Ju-bel ein!__ Ja, wer auch nur ei - ne See-le

wer ein hol-des Weib er-rungen, mische sei-nen Ju-bel ein!__ Ja, wer auch nur ei - ne See-le

wer ein hol-des Weib er-rungen, mische seinen Ju-bel ein! Ja,__ wer auch nur ei - ne See-le

sein nennt auf dem Er-den-rund! Und__wer's nie ge-konnt, der steh - le weinend sich aus

sein nennt auf dem Er-den-rund! Und__wer's nie ge-konnt, der steh - le weinend sich aus

sein nennt auf dem Er-den-rund! Und__wer's nie ge-konnt, der steh - le weinend sich aus

sein nennt auf dem Er-den-rund! Und__wer's nie ge-konnt, der steh - le weinend sich aus

294

300

302

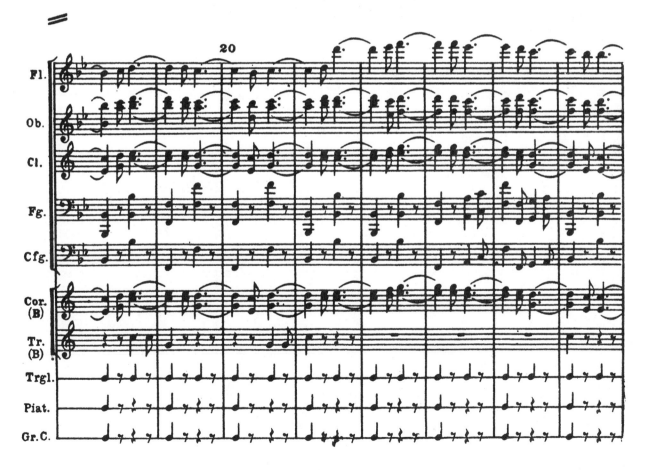

Him-mels prächt-gen Plan,   lau-fet, Brü-der, eu-re Bahn,   lau-fet,

Brü - der, eu - re Bahn, freudig, wie ein Held zum Sie - gen, wie ein

312

100

NB.(Diese 6 Takte können nicht vom Chor, wohl aber von dem Solosänger ausgelassen werden.)

freu-dig, freu-dig, wie ein Held, ein Held zum Sie-gen.

freu-dig, wie ein Held ___ zum Sie - - gen.

freu-dig, wie ein Held ___ zum Sie - - gen.

freu-dig, wie ein Held ___ zum Sie- - gen.

314

317

318

324

sanf-ter Flü - gel weilt.

sanf-ter Flü - gel weilt.

sanf-ter Flü - gel weilt.

sanf-ter Flü - gel weilt.

330

Adagio ma non troppo, ma divoto. (♩=60.)

Ü - ber Ster-nen muß er woh-nen, ü - ber

Ü - ber Ster-nen muß er woh-nen, ü - ber

Ü - ber Ster-nen muß er woh-nen,

Ü - ber Ster-nen muß er woh-nen,

336

595
60
655

Allegro energico, sempre ben marcato. (♩=84)

338

340

Freu - de!   Freu - de!

Freu - de, schö - ner Göt - ter - fun - ken, Toch - ter aus E - ly - si - um;—

— um - schlun - gen, Mil - li - o - nen!

345

350

354

356

358

359

362

Fl.
Ob.
Cl.
Fg.
Cor.
(D)
Tr.
(D)
Timp.
Vl.
Vla.
S.
A.
Chor
T.
B.
Vc.
Cb.
zu 2
p cresc.
Al - le Menschen, al - le Menschen, al - le

370

372

373

Poco allegro, stringendo il tempo, sempre più allegro.

Prestissimo. (♩ = 132)

Piccolo

2 Flauti.

2 Oboi.

2 Clarinetti in A

2 Fagotti

Contrafagotto.

4 Corni in D

2 Trombe in D

3 Tromboni { Alto e Tenore / Basso

Timpani in D-A

Triangolo

Gr. Cassa e Piatti

Violino I.

Violino II.

Viola.

Soprano

Alto

Tenore

Basso

Violoncello e Contrabasso.

CHOR.

Seid umschlungen,
Seid umschlungen,
Seid umschlungen,
Seid umschlungen,
Seid umschlungen,

E. E. 3611

Picc.
Fl.
Ob.
Cl
Fg.
Cfg.
Cor. (D)
Tr. (D)
Tbni.
Timp.
Trgl.
Piatti. Gr. C.
Vl.
Vla.
S.
Va - ter woh - - nen, ein lie - ber Va - ter
A.
Va - ter woh - - nen, ein lie - ber Va - ter
Chor
T.
Va - ter woh - - nen, ein lie - ber Va - ter
B.
Va - ter woh - - nen, ein lie - ber Va - ter
Vc Cb.

380

383

386

Maestoso. (♩=60)

387

392